It's Your Story—Tell it!

A Leadership Journey

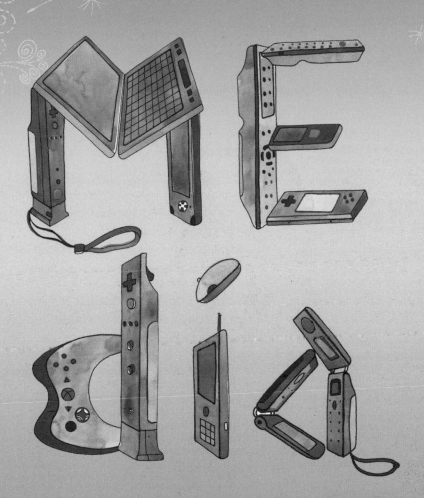

Girl Scouts of the USA

Chair,
National Board
of Directors

Connie L. Lindsey

Chief
Executive
Officer

Anna Maria Chávez

Chief
Operating
Officer

Jan Verhage

Vice
President,
Program

Eileen Doyle

girl scouts

the dove
self-esteem
fund

**PHOTOGRAPHS/BACKGROUND
IMAGES: Page 15:** Alan Markfield/20th
Century Fox, Imagewerks/Getty Images;
Page 16: Comstock/Getty Images; **Page
17:** Rian Hughes/Getty Images; **Page
20:** courtesy of Milestone Film & Video;
Page 22: Stockbyte/Getty Images; **Page
28:** David Toase/Getty Images; **Page 30:**
Rian Hughes/Getty Images; **Page 34:**
Brand X Pictures/Getty Images; **Page 35:**
Image Source/Getty Images; **Page 44:**
from the book *Comic, Comix & Graphic
Novels*, published by Phaidon Press;
Page 58: Che McPherson/Getty Images,
Michael Blann/Getty Images; **Page 70:**
Jim Spellman/Getty Images; **Page 71:**
Matthew Hertel/Getty Images; **Page 73:**
Kris Krug; **Page 85:** Dalton Rooney; **Page
86:** Rian Hughes/Getty Images; **Page 88:**
Leslie Marcus; **Page 89:** Jose Ortiz, 2009

The women mentioned in this book are
examples of how women have used their
voice in the world. This doesn't mean
that GSUSA (or you) will agree with
everything they have ever done or said.

Text printed on Fedrigoni Cento
40 percent de-inked, post-consumer
fibers and 60 percent secondary
recycled fibers.

Covers printed on Prisma artboard FSC
Certified mixed sources.

FSC
www.fsc.org

MIX
Paper from
responsible sources
FSC® C018290

This publication was made possible by a
generous grant from the Dove Self-Esteem Fund.

SENIOR DIRECTOR, PROGRAM RESOURCES: Suzanne Harper

ART DIRECTOR: Douglas Bantz

WRITERS: Wendy Thomas Russell, Sarah Goodman

CONTRIBUTORS: Valerie Takahama, Frankie Wright,
and Andrea Bastiani Archibald

EXECUTIVE EDITOR: Laura J. Tuchman

ILLUSTRATORS: Trisha Krauss, Trina Dalziel

DESIGNERS: Charlyne Fabi, Right Hat LLC, and
Pete Friedrich for Charette Communication Design

ART AND PRODUCTION: Ellen Kelliher, Sarah Micklem,
Sheryl O'Connell, Lesley Williams

© 2010 by Girl Scouts of the USA

First published in 2010 by Girl Scouts of the USA
420 Fifth Avenue, New York, NY 10018–2798
www.girlscouts.org

ISBN: 978-0-88441-752-1

Printed in Italy

3 4 5 6 7 8 9 10/18 17 16 15 14 13 12

Contents

MEdia! Cool, Crazy, and Just for You!

What's not to love about media?

You can enjoy it anytime, anywhere, for hours and hours—movies, TV, music, txts, virtual worlds, blogs, tweets!

But have you ever wondered how much of your life you're spending in someone else's reality? When you glance at a billboard, open a magazine, settle in for a movie, or surf the Web, you're really reading someone else's story.

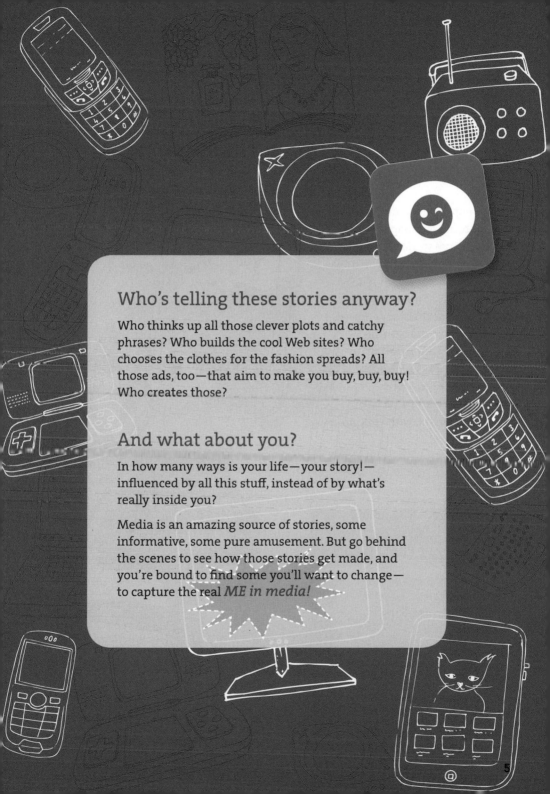

Who's telling these stories anyway?

Who thinks up all those clever plots and catchy phrases? Who builds the cool Web sites? Who chooses the clothes for the fashion spreads? All those ads, too—that aim to make you buy, buy, buy! Who creates those?

And what about you?

In how many ways is your life—your story!— influenced by all this stuff, instead of by what's really inside you?

Media is an amazing source of stories, some informative, some pure amusement. But go behind the scenes to see how those stories get made, and you're bound to find some you'll want to change— to capture the real *ME in media!*

That's where MEdia comes in.

This journey is all about you and your relationship with this great, big, multimedia world.

Meet Gadget Girl!

As you explore how all those media stories get shaped, you'll see how those stories can shape you—your thoughts and feelings about yourself and everything around you. Then you'll see how you can shape the story—for yourself, your community, your world! **That is what being a leader is all about!** It's being someone who knows herself and uses her skills to make the world better.

Post a Comment   Close X

Size: 12 ▾   **B** *I* U A   SEND

What kinds of media do you like the most? How does the media you use match the media you prefer?

Laptop to cell
freinds / friends
news
popularity / popularity

This journey is your chance to make media *and* remake media—into your true *ME*dia! Your confidence will soar as you start living *your story* instead of someone else's. You'll decide what to upload to your memory. You'll choose what to send straight to your spam folder. And you'll be the one to answer this question: What new media might you create that's nowhere yet to be found?

As you share your MEdia story and get others to join in that story, **you'll be a media leader!** And that's so much more powerful, but just as much fun, as being a media lover.

So turn the page! Get started on a MEdia story all your own!

Meet Lily Tranquillity!

I LOVE MEDIA! AND WHY NOT? MEDIA IS MY FUN ZONE, MY GO-TO PLACE FOR 411, AND MY LINK TO GAZILLIONS OF INTERESTING PEOPLE.

YEAH, BUT MEDIA CAN BE SO CONFUSING. SOMETIMES IT'S HARD TO FIGURE OUT WHAT'S TRUE AND WHAT'S NOT. AND IT'S SUCH A TIME DRAIN! GOTTA RUN—I'M OFF TO A YOGA RETREAT!

The Scoop on Journey Awards

You'll have the chance to earn three prestigious leadership awards along this journey:

MONITOR, INFLUENCE, and CULTIVATE.

To earn the **MONITOR** award, you will complete three activities that get you to hone in on the role media plays in your life and the lives of those around you, plus one that considers media in your community. Just look for the **Monitor** award icons throughout the journey, choose the activities you want to do, and fill in your Award Tracker on page 92 as you go.

To earn the **INFLUENCE** award, you will—you guessed it!—influence people in positive ways by teaming with your sister Cadettes to change media for the better through a MEdia Remake. This is your chance to put some real ME in media. Look for the **Influence** award icon on page 74, and log your efforts in your Award Tracker on page 94.

The **CULTIVATE** award is all about you cultivating a new perspective on media. To earn it, you'll challenge yourself to make a positive change in the way you use media in your life—a change that you Cultivate so it grows into full-fledged inspiration for others. Look for the **Cultivate** award icon on page 91, and log your personal media commitment, how you express it, and how you share it in your Award Tracker on page 95.

The Scoop on Scoop

"Scoop" is a journalism term meaning an exclusive—news that is reported first by one person or news organization.

If you haven't already noticed, these awards—Monitor, Influence, and Cultivate—come together to spell MIC (short for microphone).

Together they give you a way to broadcast—to amplify—your own story. Each award gets you one step closer to the **MIC!**

OOH, A MIC! COUNT ME IN!

Setting Your Sights on Silver?

Earning these MEdia journey awards will give you the skills you need to plan and carry out a Silver Award project that moves you up the Girl Scout leadership ladder!

Want to Earn a LiA?

Earn a Leader in Action award by giving an assist to a Brownie group taking a Girl Scout leadership journey. You'll boost your leadership skills and share your knowledge.

Ask an adult volunteer for assistance locating a Brownie group that would love to have your unique talents and skills on tap!

Media = Communication

What exactly is media? Good question! Here's the short answer: Media refers to all the tools used to communicate with many people at once. Think books, magazines, newspapers. Think TV and radio. Think advertisements on a bus bench—or on a bus! Think fliers stuck under a windshield wiper, or giant videos on the sides of buildings. Think movies. Think blogs. Think social media.

Media is everywhere. It's out there raising your awareness about the world, and informing your decisions. It's trying to persuade you to do things and care about things you may not need to do or care about. It's constantly telling you what's right and what's true and what's hip.

Pretty major, right?

VERY!

Post a Comment

Close ☒

Size: 12 ▾   B *I* U A   SEND

What does media mean to you? How does it sway you?

Slice the Media Pie

Think about how much media you consume each day. Do you swallow it in bits or take huge bites? If the pie below represents your daily media intake, how would you slice it? If you're a big-time Web surfer, the largest piece might go to the Internet. TV will get a sizable chunk of your pie if you spend hours in front of the tube.

INTERNET

PHONE

BOOKS

▶ Slice and label your pie, then talk it over with your friends or family members. What do they think about your media consumption? How does it compare to their own?

MOVIES

NEWSPAPERS

GAMES
(on phones, computers, video)

TELEVISION

MUSIC
(radio, downloads)

MAGAZINES

How Much Is Too Much?

Your MEdia Meter Rating

Media is everywhere.
But how much you engage with it
depends on who you are, what you enjoy,
and your priorities.

How important is media to you?

Take THIS quiz and FIND out!

dB

－   ＋

To take another fun media quiz, visit ForGirls.GirlScouts.org and
click on "Activities" in the Girls 10–12 age category.

Someone asks you how many text messages you received today. You answer:

A. Texts? I don't even have a cell phone!
B. Let me go check...
C. 2 many 2 count

When taking a trip, you:

A. Spend your time people-watching and chatting with your companions.
B. Put your cell phone on "vibrate" and take a book along for the ride.
C. Make sure your laptop is fully charged, fill your backpack with magazines, and turn up the music on your MP3 to drown out the sounds of everyone around you.

School is canceled because of snow. You:

A. Pile on winter clothes and spend the day sledding, skiing, snowboarding, or ice-skating.
B. Catch a movie with your best pals.
C. Retreat to your room for a day of online chatting with your friends.

How much TV do you watch on a typical Saturday?

A. The TV might as well be broken for how little I watch it.
B. Depends what's on.
C. Impossible to say. The TV is on all the time in the background.

When you go to school on a Monday, how much do you already know about what your friends did over the weekend?

A. Nothing! Wouldn't that just take the fun out of Monday morning chatter?
B. I'm on a need-to-know basis with my friends. If it's important, they'll call.
C. I know everything there is to know, and more. That's why social media was invented, right?

Turn the page to see how you did!

Count your answers,

giving 1 point for all A answers,
2 points for B answers,
and 3 points for C answers.

Between 5 and 7 points:
You prefer to live in the real world, thank you very much.
Lily Tranquillity would be proud . . . but Gadget Girl wouldn't!
How do you keep up with what's going on?

Between 8 and 12:
Congratulations! You live and breathe the motto "Everything
in moderation." Still, make sure your habits stay healthy by
balancing what you expose yourself to. For every 15 minutes
you spend on a social media site, spend 15 minutes reading
the news, or watching a documentary, or researching a
Girl Scout project!

Between 13 and 15:
You may be dangerously close to developing a condition
known as Gadget Girl-itis. It may be time to take a
Lily Tranquillity break!

So how much media really is too much?

It's a hard question to nail because media time—surfing to find the answer to a
question like this one, for example—can be put to good use, too. Media can take
you places that deepen your knowledge, heighten your creativity, and enrich
your life!

The truth is, only you can be the judge of how much is too much. Because only
you know how much quality time you're spending with media, and how much
of it is having a positive influence on your life!

Ms. Multi-Media!

Selena Gomez has been acting since she was 7, and her celebrity spans many media.

She's well known for playing a teen wizard on TV, and her movie career includes a turn as the older sister in *Ramona and Beezus*, which is based on the book series by Beverly Cleary.

She's been a spokesperson for a milk producer in print and TV ads, and appeared in a back-to-school fashion TV ad campaign for a major department store. She's the singer in her own band, Selena Gomez & the Scene. And as the youngest UNICEF ambassador ever, she traveled to raise awareness of the needs of children in Ghana, Africa.

But whatever Selena does, she puts something of herself in it. "I feel like every character I put myself into is a part of me in some shape or form," she says.

Take her role as Beezus, big sister of Ramona Quimby. Even though Selena is an only child, she grew up surrounded by younger children, thanks to her grandmother, who helped to raise her. "I grew up around a lot of kids, and watched my grandmother treat them with love," she says.

These days, Selena recognizes that she is a role model for young girls. It's another part that she takes on with confidence. "I understand that there are girls who are going to look up to me. I guess that means it's my job to be the best that I can be for the kids and for myself," she says.

Amazing Media!

Nobody needs to tell you that technology is constantly changing.

You've watched MP3 players get smaller and smaller. You've seen cell phones get more and more elaborate. Still, it's hard to grasp how quickly things change. Every few months, it seems, there's some new must-have on the high-tech horizon. And every few months, something old drops off the map. What's super-hot today will be as boring as black-and-white TV to your grandkids.

(Can you believe black-and-white TV was once the cool, new thing?)

File Under "Appreciation"

When it comes to the media, chances are good that you have a lot to be grateful for. Name four ways in which the media has entertained, educated, or inspired you.

1.
2.
3.
4.

1984

The first cell phone is out! It weighs 2 pounds, measures 13 inches long by 3 inches wide, and sells for nearly $4,000—which is why not many people own one. Today's cell phones are more like sleek computers in your hand. Check your e-mail, surf the Internet. *No wonder they're called smartphones!*

2007

E-readers enter the scene, changing the way books are bought, carried, and shared.

THE NEXT BiG THING

Necessity is the mother of invention. That is, people invent things because they need them. (Or they think they do!) What do you think the next "new thing" will be? What will the next generation of kids be salivating over?

Now, how about sketching it— or building it?

Media Job Listing

Media product designer

A person who comes up with ideas and then develops those ideas into full-fledged, working objects and services for the media industry. Product designers are responsible for computers, gadgets, software, cell phone apps, and a ton of other cool stuff.

The Media's Seven-Layer Dip

Have you ever watched TV online?

Or heard a blogger being interviewed on the radio?

Or read about a movie in the newspaper?

Sometimes, the media seems like ingredients in a seven-layer dip—all joined together and impossible to separate. Not only are newspapers, magazines, TV shows, music, and movies now online, but what happens online feeds other media, too.

A story might be published on a Web site and later covered by a newspaper, which then creates a feeding frenzy among TV stations.

A podcast might make it onto the radio.

A blogger might sign a movie deal.

New media reports on old media.

Old media covers every new thing about new media!

Web sites "talk" about other Web sites.

And the list goes on! News is shared and transferred so many times that the true meaning sometimes gets lost altogether, like a giant game of telephone!

Dip into the Dip!

Find three examples of how media interconnects with other media—how an idea or story spreads throughout the seven-layer dip. Figure out why it was spread in the first place, and ask yourself how it tastes!

Toward the Award

 ①

②

③

A Real Seven-Layer Dip

1 16-ounce can refried beans
1 jar salsa
1 16-ounce can black beans, drained
2 cups sour cream
2 cups chopped avocados
2 tablespoons lime juice
2 plum tomatoes, diced
1 cup green olives, chopped

Layer the refried beans, salsa, and black beans in a small, deep casserole dish. Microwave on high until heated through. Combine the avocados and lime juice. Layer the avocado mixture and the sour cream on the warm beans, then top with diced tomatoes and olives.

Serve with low-sodium tortilla chips, whole-grain crackers, or vegetable "scoops" (peppers, jicama, celery, etc.).

Animation Then and Now

The oldest surviving animated feature film? Lotte Reiniger's 1926 *The Adventures of Prince Achmed*, from the *Arabian Nights* tales. Reiniger, a cut-paper pioneer, worked in the film industry making title cards for silent movies. But her passion for making cut-paper silhouettes led her to tell full stories in film, too.

She would film cut-out figures in front of a white background one frame at a time. This cut-paper technique of hers has been borrowed by many animated films through the years. Search on Reiniger's name to view her back-lit paper puppet animation on the Web.

And did you know that those amazing animation scenes in the 2009 movie *Avatar* took 14 years to produce? Twelve of them went to developing a new camera system that combined live actors and fantasy effects. To tell YOUR stories, you can use some simple animation effects that won't take years!

Check out the ideas along this journey (on the opposite page and on pages 47 and 67) and share them with friends. Try one or two—or all three!

Media Job Listing

Animator
An artist who designs images that, when rapidly displayed, create an illusion of movement called "animation." Animators can work in film, TV, video games, and on the Web.

Anim-8

Moving Pictures

Here's a low-tech way to make a moving picture:

1. Start with an unlined memo pad. Wrap masking tape tightly around the top inch of the pad.

2. Using only the bottom half of the page—and only one line!—quickly draw a simple picture on the last page of the pad (examples: a circle, a seed, a balloon, an ice-cream cone).

3. Let the next-to-last page of the pad drop, so it covers the back page. Then trace over your first picture, but change it slightly. If you drew a circle, for example, now add a facial feature to it. Or make your seed sprout, or your ice-cream cone melt a little.

4. Keep tracing, page by page, changing your drawing slightly each time for at least 24 pages.

5. Now hold the top of the pad with your left (or non-dominant) hand and use your drawing hand to flip the pages quickly with your thumb. Flip through several times to get the pictures moving evenly at a speed you like.

And the
Award
Goes to...

the
Girl
Scouts?

National Headquarters Girl Scouts
presents

The Golden Eaglet.
The Story
of a
Girl Scout.
Copyright 1918 National Headquarters Girl Scouts

Every Girl Scout knows how to tie a number of knots, from a Clove Hitch to a Sheet Bend.

Have you ever watched a silent film?

That is, a film without spoken dialogue—only printed words and background music? In the early 1900s, silent films were the only movies being made.

Well, get this: In 1918—when women hiked mountains in floor-length skirts!—Girl Scouts founder Juliette Gordon Low produced a silent film called *The Golden Eaglet*. It was named for the highest honor a Girl Scout could receive back then. The film shows girls doing all sorts of cool things—camping, fire-starting, first-aid—and ends by urging people to start their own troop.

During her lifetime, Low was the focus of plenty of media attention. Articles were written about her, and she made the newsreels, too. But she always managed to use the media much more than she was used by it! *The Golden Eaglet* proves just that!

1897

The world's first movie house is built in Paris. Exactly 100 years later, a new film-based industry would emerge: Netflix!

Look for more **Take a Media Moment** tickets along this journey!

126513

126514

Take a Media Moment

Yes, media can be all-consuming—and overwhelming. But don't ever forget that media can be rejuvenating, too! Take movies, for example. They can be wonderfully relaxing—a great escape! In fact, movie ticket sales spiked during the Great Depression, when people flocked to theaters for a break from reality. It's no coincidence that the 1930s were a heyday of lavish movie musicals, screwball comedies, and fast-paced romantic comedies with glamorous stars like Carole Lombard and Cary Grant. So take time to see one. Old movies can be loads of cool, campy fun!

POP CORN

1939
A most outstanding year for motion pictures. **Three movies in color** are introduced to wide audiences. One, "The Wizard of Oz," is now a TV favorite.

1972
Videocassette movies are now for rent in video stores. And that was supposed to be the end of movie theaters. Guess not!

Archive This, Trash That

Part of the media's job is to throw images at you to get you to react.

It's your job to screen what you see—to separate the positive from the negative, the helpful from the harmful, fact from fiction. When it comes to media and your life, it's up to you to screen out what's inaccurate or misleading, what might be making you believe something you really shouldn't believe.

Consider the Source

A classmate you barely know approaches you at school and whispers something about another girl—who happens to be your best friend! You know that something is just gossip; it's not true. But others don't know your friend the way you do.

Sometimes, media messages are no more trustworthy than your school's rumor mill. Yet you might assume that those expensive beauty products being advertised really remove acne overnight or that those ring tones are really free...but that may not be the case.

Ads are full of words that are meant to sell something, not words that present the facts. You can accept those messages or screen them out. Or you can take the matter into your own hands and learn the truth—the key is to consider the source! That doesn't sound too hard, until you consider how many ads are thrown at you each day...

Sound Bite

Urban legends and other misinformation

The Internet is a breeding ground for "urban legends," which are false stories told as if true. Next time you receive a text or e-mail about something that seems unbelievable, confirm it before you spread it.

Messages and Their Meaning

Lots of people make money by delivering "messages" that are meant to sell you products or services.

People also create messages to sell you on the idea of something, like what's good to think or do (in their opinion), or the kind of image you should present to others (again, in their opinion).

> Think about all the advertising messages you've seen today.

Keep in mind that all media messages aren't bad. Media messages do a world of good—raising awareness of worthy causes, alerting people to dangers, and getting the word out about all kinds of important things.

Fliers on a bulletin board.

Ads on the radio, billboards, placards on a subway or bus, TV jingles you can't get out of your head.

Ads that pop up on Web sites or play before a movie...well, you get the picture.

Sound Bite

Public service announcements, or PSAs, are basically ads designed to raise awareness about important issues—like telling people about health risks.

The shopping cart handle ("grab-ertising") and the store intercom telling you about the latest deal—those are messages, too!

My Day of Message OVERLOAD!

Toward the Award

monitor

All the junk mail in your snail mailbox—those are messages.

For one day, track all the ad messages you see, from when you wake up to when you go to sleep. Then take a long look at your (long!) list. What exactly are all these messages trying to sell you or say to you? How do you feel about what the ads show as "desirable"— what success or popularity or beauty looks like? And how would you feel about what the ads show if you were another type of girl from another background?

Write what you think about the **number** of messages you see in a day, too. How has your view of those ads changed now that you've taken time to think about their messages?

Post a Comment   Close X

Size: 12 ▾   B I U A   SEND

Advertising in disguise? Watch one TV show or movie. Count every time you see or hear something meant to make you buy, want, or believe something.

Getting Hooked

Have you ever been so "hooked" by an ad that you can't get it out of your head?

Ads are cleverly designed to grab your attention, build your trust, and make you want to buy, or buy into, something. Advertisers call these "persuasion techniques." Here are six of the most common. (Which do you recognize? Which are easiest to resist?)

Association: Links a product, service, or idea with something people want, like happiness, comfort, or safety.

Bribery: Promises you something else, such as a rebate or "free" gift, if you buy the product.

Get on the Bandwagon: Shows lots of people enjoying a product, with the hope that you won't want to be left out.

The Beautiful People: Features good-looking models in fashionable clothes and places to grab your attention.

Fear: Links a product, service, or idea to a "solution" to something people fear, like bad breath or higher taxes.

Humor: Makes you laugh. (Who doesn't want to laugh?)

1926

The first radio jingle airs, for Wheaties. It starts like this:

Have you tried Wheaties?
They're whole wheat with all of the bran.
Won't you try Wheaties?
For wheat is the best food of man...

More than 80 years later, whole grains are still being touted—everywhere! But, "man," this jingle wouldn't fly today, would it?

Next time you're hooked by an ad or commercial, take a closer look. What exactly do you like about it? What persuasion technique is being used? How does it play on your desires or fears?

Now that you've analyzed its persuasion technique, do you see the ad and its product in a new way?

What about the ad might you want to change for the better?

Media Job Listing

Advertising Copywriter

A person who writes the copy for advertising. Her job is to persuade people to purchase products or services, or support political candidates or ideas.

SPOT the Product

TV and movies are notorious for "product placement"—planting brand-name products in scenes to advertise them.

Product placement can involve anything from laptops to cereal to sneakers. Ever notice a character in a movie grabbing lunch at a burger chain? Or how about the soft drinks the judges sip on those grueling reality talent shows? Watch your favorite show and take note of what the characters are drinking, eating, wearing, and driving. How many brand names can you spot?

~~~~~~

~~~~~~

~~~~~~

~~~~~~

~~~~~~

Make a Game of It!

Have some fun spotting persuasion techniques and/or product placements with friends, sister Cadettes, or family members. **Who can spot the most** in an hour, in a day, during a car ride—or during one episode of one prime-time TV show?

Sound Bite

"Advergaming" is the practice of using video games to advertise products. The term is also used when companies create free games for their Web sites.

Logo Evolution

A logo is considered the "face" of a company. It's a symbol that is instantly recognizable. And it sums up in a simple visual what the company stands for.

Take a look at this logo.

HALOID

Q. Do you have any idea what company it represents?

Turn the page!
—you might be surprised!

A. Xerox!

1906   1958   1968   *Current logo*

Xerox was founded in 1906 as "The Haloid Photographic Company," which manufactured photographic paper and equipment. The company changed its name to "Haloid Xerox" in 1958 and then simply "Xerox" in 1961. See how the logos switch from Haloid to Haloid-Xerox to Xerox?

Now, take a look at each of these logo evolutions and try to spot the reasons they changed—or didn't change, as the case may be.

1914   1921   1932

1941   1956   1968

Then ask yourself:

- Should logos really matter that much?

- Is it just like judging a book by its cover, or judging a person by the way she looks rather than what's inside?

- Why or why not?

> Now, take a look at the Girl Scouts logo on the next page.

Notice how Girl Scouts has changed its look over the years.

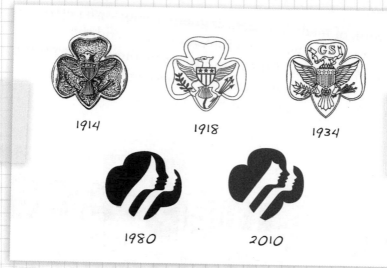

1914 1918 1934

1980 2010

What other logos catch your eye?

Which ones make you stop and take a longer look?

What about them do you like?

How about the ads made for these brands?

How do they lure you in—or turn you off?

Cut out some logos you really like from magazines and paste one or a few of them here. Then perform a media-sage/culture-critic analysis of them by asking yourself why you like them. After you answer, ask yourself why again! Keep asking why! You'll be amazed how far you can go in figuring out the many subtle ways that logos work.

Your Media Guest List

Think of media messages as guests at your own party.
You can invite them into your home and chat
them up for hours. Or you can never let them in the door.
The point is that you are in control of your story—
and your media world.

Toward the Award

mESsAGEs in the Girl Scout Law

The Girl Scout Law is full of messages! The Law is basically a 52-word sentence with 16 inspiring messages! Count 'em!

The Law has been spread both through word of mouth and the media. It's been repeated countless times in magazines, books, brochures, and—of course—online. If you have access to the Internet, search "Girl Scout Law" and see how many results you get!

Now the challenge!
Find three examples of media, anywhere around you, that support the Girl Scout Law. Share them with your friends.

① binder GS

②

③

1921
Skywriting. Ooh!

1923
Neon Signs. Ahh!

Be a Spam Blocker!

Don't you wish you had a spam folder built right into your brain? You'd never have to see another annoying ad or commercial.

Unfortunately, blocking media and its messages requires a bit more effort. But it can be fun, too.

Try one of these "blocking" activities:

Trash to Treasure:

Go through an old magazine or newspaper and clip anything meant to get you (or anyone) to buy or believe something. Then decide which of the clippings you would want to "trash." Go ahead—cut them up, shred them! Put them back together in a new way. What kind of statement can you make? Or what object can you build? Create something you'd want to archive forever. (This is definitely one way to turn trash into treasure!)

Blocked a pile of ads?

How many? _____

Turned them into a message to keep:
(Describe it!)

~~~~~~~~~~~~~~~~~~~~~~~~~~
~~~~~~~~~~~~~~~~~~~~~~~~~~
~~~~~~~~~~~~~~~~~~~~~~~~~~
~~~~~~~~~~~~~~~~~~~~~~~~~~
~~~~~~~~~~~~~~~~~~~~~~~~~~
~~~~~~~~~~~~~~~~~~~~~~~~~~
~~~~~~~~~~~~~~~~~~~~~~~~~~
~~~~~~~~~~~~~~~~~~~~~~~~~~
~~~~~~~~~~~~~~~~~~~~~~~~~~
~~~~~~~~~~~~~~~~~~~~~~~~~~
~~~~~~~~~~~~~~~~~~~~~~~~~~
~~~~~~~~~~~~~~~~~~~~~~~~~~
~~~~~~~~~~~~~~~~~~~~~~~~~~

Menu of Options

Making choices, online or in life, is easier when you slow down, step back, and use your head. When deciding whether to do something, ask yourself these questions:

Why do I want to do this?	▶
What are the pros and cons?	▶
Could this endanger my health, hurt someone else, or injure my credibility?	▶
What is my gut instinct?	▶
Does this feel right to me?	▶

When did you last slow down, step back, and make a decision you were really proud of?	▶
Give it a try when you next have the chance.	▶
Note how it goes!	▼

Time Out! ⊗   TMI!   ⊗

Have you ever posted details of your life, or someone else's, and had the posts come back to haunt you?

The Internet is BIGGER than your school, your city, and your country. It's a vast web of connections in which information can be stored and recalled long after it's "deleted."

So being cautious is just plain smart. If you wouldn't post it on your front door, don't post it online! Set your e-communications to the same standards you set in real life. Treat those you chat with the same way you would a person you only "kind of know."

Sometimes too much information is just Too Much Information!

Phone-a-Friend

On TV game shows, a "phone-a-friend" is a person contestants can call to get help with trivia questions. In real life, a "phone-a-friend" is someone you trust completely and can count on to help you make good, healthy decisions. Who's yours?

Every girl needs a trusted adult in her corner, too. Whether it's your mom, your aunt, a friend of the family, or a teacher at school, a trusted adult can offer wisdom, guidance, and a fresh (and wise) perspective.

Advice I could use
most right now: ~~~~~~~~~~~~~~~~~~~~

My trusted adult: ~~~~~~~~~~~~~~~~~~~~

Navigating Your Story

Sometimes life can seem like a maze of obstacles—at school, in friendships, in family life. If you're looking for some great ways to navigate that maze, check out the leadership journey *aMAZE!* It's all about navigating the twists and turns of relationships.

And if you are soon to be a Girl Scout Senior, check out *GIRLtopia*, the leadership journey that invites Seniors to imagine a perfect world for girls —for you, your friends, and all girls everywhere!

YOU KNOW ONE THING I'M GOOD AT? THINKING FOR MYSELF. PEER PRESSURE IS SO LAST YEAR.

I'M LIKING YOU MORE AND MORE! WOULD YOU BE MY PHONE-A-FRIEND?

ARE YOU KIDDING? I'D LOVE TO! YOU CAN CALL ME ON MY CELL!

Toeing the Line

No person is entirely "objective," and that means that no media is entirely objective either. But that word is used a lot to draw lines between certain types of media.

News reporters try to stay neutral and keep their personal opinions and emotions to themselves when they gather or report facts. Their job is to inform by giving you a balanced view of what is going on.

Columnists, editorial writers, and bloggers offer their own opinions, observations, or slants. Their job is to persuade you, by getting you to see things their way.

From your experience, how would you label the following media: objective, slanted, or both? Why?

	objective	slanted	both	Why?
Fruit-drink commercial				
Health and exercise blog				
Fashion column				
Radio news				
Fashion spread in a magazine				

http://www.soyouwannablog.com/   RSS ⟳

SO YOU WANNA BLOG?

Imagine you are hired to be a blogger who can blog about whatever you want—as long as you blog every day and have a new blog posted by noon.

Posted at 10:52 a.m.   2 comments

Would you blog about:

:: the little <u>details</u> of your life
:: what you ate for <u>breakfast</u>
:: where you took your <u>dog</u> for a walk,
:: what you <u>wrote</u> in your diary?

. . . Or would you blog about world issues and current events? In what ways could you use your blog to <u>educate and inspire</u> others on issues of concern to you?

Posted at 11:23 a.m.   0 comments

Would you blog about the same kinds of things each day, or would you <u>switch it up</u>?

Who do you think would read your blog? How would they first <u>find out</u> about it?

Would you let companies advertise on your blog? If so, what kinds of <u>advertisements</u> would you accept? What would these advertisements say about you?

Media Job Listing **Blogger** A person who posts a blog (short for Web log) for fun or for work. Some bloggers write personal opinions, some share information or comment on events, and some simply chronicle their daily life. The blogosphere is free—one reason blogs are so numerous!

2002

Blogs show up on the Internet. Within five years, more than 112 million blogs are tracked, and the number keeps growing. That's a lot of people telling their story, and putting their ME in media!

When Reality Isn't Real

Reality TV has made countless celebrities out of virtual "nobodies." But reality TV isn't reality. "It's probably the most scripted television in Los Angeles," says TV producer Melissa Freeman Fuller.

Fuller has seen crew members set up situations, feed lines to the participants, plant people in scenes, and edit shots to make them appear more dramatic or interesting. She could give dozens of examples, but the most extreme are from her time filming a TV series about the drama of running a large hotel in Las Vegas.

To accomplish this, many scenes had to be invented or embellished. The crew, including Fuller, told cast members how to act and what to say. Even when a wedding cake accidentally dropped on the floor, the crew asked that it be done again—to get a better shot. They even asked the people involved to change their reactions.

2000

Reality TV shows like *Survivor* are big hits in the States and soon become big business. How many of your favorite stars came from the ranks of reality TV?

Melissa Freeman Fuller

Inventive tactics continued in the editing rooms, where people's quotes were taken out of context or spliced together to make them fulfill whatever "role" the show needed. "You can be the nicest person in the world. But by the time we cut you up, you're a monster," Fuller says. (The term coined for this practice is "Franken-editing," after Victor Frankenstein, the monster-making scientist in Mary Shelley's novel *Frankenstein*.)

Not all shows are so highly produced, but "the demand for shock value has made the industry do some pretty shameless things to boost ratings," Fuller says. These days, though, she rarely watches.

Melissa Freeman Fuller's Career Path:

After 12 years in the industry—first as a camera assistant for both TV and film, then as a camera operator, producer, and writer for numerous shows—Fuller decided to leave Hollywood and open a production company in Lincoln, Nebraska, with her husband.

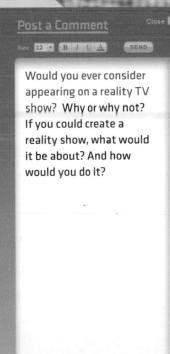

Post a Comment   Close ✖

Size: 12 ▾   **B** *I* U A   SEND

Would you ever consider appearing on a reality TV show? Why or why not? If you could create a reality show, what would it be about? And how would you do It?

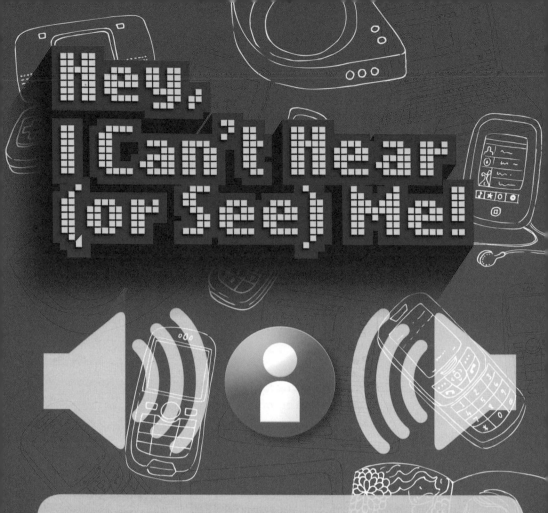

Hey, I Can't Hear (or See) Me!

Think about all the people behind the media, and how every one of them is trying to accomplish something—that's a lot of people chattering at you all at once.

Sometimes it can be hard to hear your own voice over all that noise! It's time to think about how all those voices are affecting your feelings and emotions—and whether you want them to!

Dialing into Stereotypes

Part 1: All of Us

When you judge other people based on a common characteristic, it's called stereotyping. And, unfortunately, there's a lot of stereotyping in the world, including in media. Can you identify which characteristics are being stereotyped in the following statements?

(A) He's too old to do that job.

(B) Poor people don't try hard enough.

(C) We should feel sorry for him because he's in a wheelchair.

(D) If she'd just stop eating so much, she could be thin.

Answers: A. age, B. money, C. disabilities, D. weight

Part 2: Just Girls

Which of these statements are stereotypes?

(A) Girls love pink.

(B) Girls live to shop.

(C) Girls think makeovers can fix all their problems.

(D) Girls believe that having a boyfriend is more important than having girlfriends.

(E) Math and science are too hard for girls, or they just don't like those subjects.

(F) Girls only use the computer to chat with friends.

Answer: All of them! And there are probably more you can name!

What the Experts Say

The Entman-Rojecki Index of Race and the Media reports that black girls are inaccurately depicted as violent in movies far more than white girls.

The Umbrella Project, a Swedish organization that raises awareness about diversity, points out that when movies are made about people with disabilities, the disabilities are generally a major focus. A person who is paralyzed, for instance, is rarely treated the same way as a person with leg braces or who temporarily requires crutches to walk.

According to the Council on Size & Weight Discrimination, overweight people on sitcoms are often shown "eating constantly" and are portrayed as "lazy and stupid."

1896
The first comic strip, "The Yellow Kid," appears in a newspaper. It features a bald, snaggle-toothed child in a yellow nightshirt who hangs around a ghetto alley with other odd characters.

Stereotypes:

Easy but Inaccurate

People stereotype because it makes things easy. Stereotypes let people mistakenly assume they have a "handle" on how a certain group of people believe or behave.

Advertisers stereotype by lumping people into a group and targeting their messages to that group.

Has an ad ever convinced you that you "belong" to a certain group of people and therefore should want something or buy something because of it? As in, "I'm a fashionable person, therefore I need the most current fashions."

If you are careful to view yourself as an individual and put stereotypes aside, you have an extra level of protection against messages that aren't really about you—or for you. That's taking control of your story!

WHEN SOME PEOPLE HEAR I'M A VEGETARIAN. THEY CALL ME A "TREE HUGGER." BUT I'VE NEVER ONCE HUGGED A TREE! I DON'T EVEN LIKE TO HIKE!

AT LEAST NO ONE ASSUMES YOU'RE A GEEK!

HOW'D WE GET THESE NAMES, ANYWAY?

ARE WE STEREOTYPES?

YA THINK? WELL, AT LEAST WE'RE IN THIS JOURNEY. THAT'S COOL.

Stereotype Search

- Find two ads for the same kind of product (razors, shampoos, shoes, medicines), one with a man, another with a woman. <u>Compare the ads.</u>

- Find two ads that portray people from various social classes—drill down a little and look at professionals (doctors, scientists) versus "blue collar" workers (construction or maintenance workers). <u>Compare the ads.</u>

- Find two ads that feature people of various races or nationalities. Again, <u>compare ads</u> for a similar product.

- And finally: Who isn't being portrayed at all in advertising? Who can't you find? <u>Why?</u>

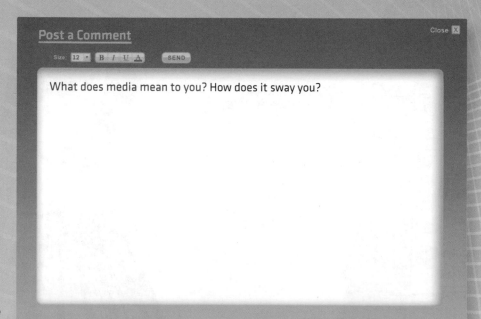

Post a Comment   Close ☒

Size: 12 ▾ B I U A   SEND

What does media mean to you? How does it sway you?

Anim-8
Spin it

Ever heard of a thaumatrope or "turning wonder"? It's a toy from the 1800s that combines two drawn images into one. You can make a thaumatrope with two index cards, a marker, strong clear tape, and a pencil or chopstick. Your image will bounce, wiggle, flap, or shimmy as it changes between the two cards.

1. Start with two index cards.

2. Decide on an idea for a simple figure doing a simple action—such as a bird lifting its wings, a frog jumping, or a snake wiggling.

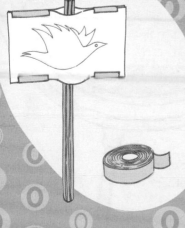

3. Draw the figure in two positions (such as wings up, wings down).

4. Tape the two cards together (images facing out) over the pencil or chopstick.

If you're earning your LiA award, try making some with your Brownie group!

5. Make the picture "move" by spinning the pencil or chopstick back and forth.

Your Body, Your Friend

It's natural to compare your looks to other girls' looks, whether they're girls who sit next to you in class or girls you see on TV. But when it comes to looks, lots of girls are hard on themselves—way too hard!

What if your body was your sister or your best friend? Would you ever criticize your best friend's physical appearance? Of course not!

If you think of your body as a cherished friend, you'll be patient with her and kind to her. You'll tell her she looks great and remind her that you love her just the way she is. You'll thank her for toting around all your schoolbooks or helping you climb the stairs. You'll pat her on the back for allowing you to hug your mom and tickle your little brother. Maybe you'll even take her out dancing. Lucky girl!

Now give it a try!

Each morning for a week, tell this best friend of yours—yourself—how great she looks. Record what you say and how it makes you feel.

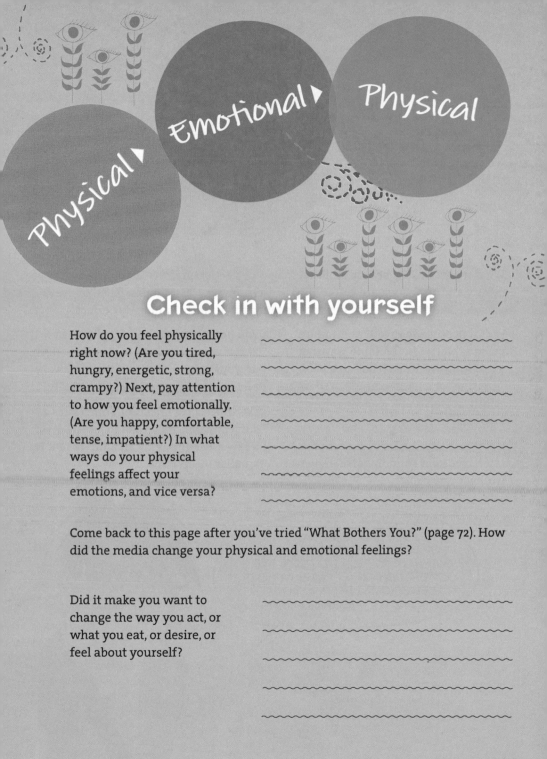

Physical ▶

Emotional ▶

Physical

Check in with yourself

How do you feel physically right now? (Are you tired, hungry, energetic, strong, crampy?) Next, pay attention to how you feel emotionally. (Are you happy, comfortable, tense, impatient?) In what ways do your physical feelings affect your emotions, and vice versa?

Come back to this page after you've tried "What Bothers You?" (page 72). How did the media change your physical and emotional feelings?

Did it make you want to change the way you act, or what you eat, or desire, or feel about yourself?

"Who Says?" Time to Talk Back!

What makes beauty beautiful? What makes perfection prefect? Whose standards of beauty and perfection are you trying to reach, anyway? Isn't it possible that every person—like every cloud in the sky—is uniquely beautiful, uniquely perfect?

Isn't it possible that you might find a person "pretty" in the same way that you'd find a Web site "cool" or a book "exciting" or a movie "funny"? These are clearly personal preferences, rather than universal truths.

Unfortunately, the media's preferences often come out sounding like universal truths.

You probably have some basic ideas about what you think is beautiful. How do your ideas differ from the media's or anyone else's?

OK, that's a big question. Sometimes a subject seems too broad to just dash off a few quick thoughts about it. Take it in smaller pieces.

IF I SEE ANOTHER BEAUTY AD POP UP ON MY SCREEN, I THINK I MAY HAVE TO PULL THE PLUG. I'VE GOT ENOUGH ON MY PLATE WITHOUT BEING TOLD I NEED TO LOOK "PRETTY" ALL THE TIME!

Here's one way: For each letter in "beauty," think of things that start with that letter that you think are beautiful. Butterfly? Beagle? Bike? Let those words trigger YOUR thoughts about what is beautiful to you and why.

Now have some fun talking back

" *I don't need to wear the clothes you are selling or use the shampoo or*

~~~~~~~~~~~~~~~~~~~~~~~~~~~

or ~~~~~~~~~~~~~~~~~~~~~
you are selling or spend my money on

~~~~~~~~~~~~~~~~~~~~~~~~~~~

to feel beautiful or to know what I think is beautiful! **"**

B

E

A

U

T

Y

Take a Media Moment

Flip though a new magazine.
If you tend to pick up the same teen magazines every month, instead try one about science, business, sports, history, or travel. In the United States alone, there are about 2,000 magazines to choose from. Which ones might give you the MEdia story you're looking for?

Picture Perfect

Diana Ragland thinks of herself as part makeup artist, part plastic surgeon. She has smoothed out skin, removed pimples, softened wrinkles, brightened eyes. She has also contoured bellies, removed scars, and fixed hair.

Ragland's job is to "doctor" photographs of celebrities for magazines and advertisements. She's a photographer and graphic designer who specializes in retouching images.

"A couple dozen mouse clicks, for example, can give a model a nose job or lift a woman's eyebrows—things only plastic surgeons do in real life," Ragland says.

"Unless you know the photographs are retouched," she adds, "you probably wouldn't suspect a thing." Even when Ragland changes backgrounds—making it look like models are on African safaris when they're actually standing in studios—the photographs look authentic.

DIANA RAGLAND ▶ 05

04

How much retouching is done to a picture depends on the person, the photographer, and the publication. Ragland won't name names, though: No celebrities want to call attention to the fact that their images were retouched.

Ragland spends a lot of time retouching faces for cosmetics ads, and it's little wonder. "They are selling beauty and perfection. If you can't show a perfect complexion, then you can't sell it. And it's about sales, not realism."

Ragland, the mother of a young daughter, sometimes "feels a tinge of guilt" when she tells people what she does for a living. She tries to minimize what she terms "radical changes," but still struggles with the notion that girls might look at magazine photos and strive to attain what she calls "a beautiful illusion."

Graphic Designer

A person who blends images and typography to create a piece of design. She may work with print publications, electronic media, or in the advertising industry.

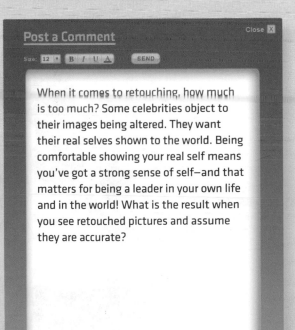

Post a Comment   Close X

Size: 12 ▾   B I U A   SEND

When it comes to retouching, how much is too much? Some celebrities object to their images being altered. They want their real selves shown to the world. Being comfortable showing your real self means you've got a strong sense of self—and that matters for being a leader in your own life and in the world! What is the result when you see retouched pictures and assume they are accurate?

Photographer

A person who takes pictures using a camera, whether a photojournalist (who photographs actual events or places in the world), fine art photographer (who takes pictures for their artistic value), or commercial photographer (who shoots products or models).

Power Down

Sleep is necessary—
for computers and for you!

Try powering down for a while. Moving away from media, even for a short time, can show you how important media is in your life and possibly inspire some balance. So unplug and reboot. Hide the newspaper, shut off the TV, power down your cell, log off the computer. Instead, have a chat with a good friend, play with your dog, go for a bike ride. Doing so might actually boost your enjoyment of media when you return to it! After all, absence makes the heart grow fonder—and maybe even healthier, too.

Time for yourself, time for fresh air

If that sounds appealing, there's another amazing Cadette leadership journey waiting for you: **Breathe**. If you haven't already, give it a try!

You might even start thinking about your time as a Girl Scout Senior, when you can dig into *Sow What?,* the leadership journey all about food that's good for you and good for the planet.

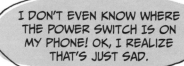

I DON'T EVEN KNOW WHERE THE POWER SWITCH IS ON MY PHONE! OK, I REALIZE THAT'S JUST SAD.

MORE ways to POWER DOWN

Go on an Adventure Weekend!

As a Girl Scout, you know that getting out in nature is a great way to fuel your body and mind. For an inspiring Adventure Weekend, dial into your natural surroundings—what you see, hear, smell, feel, taste, and think—and notice how it feels to power off for a while.

Do Some Yoga Breathing!

With your mouth closed, draw in a deep breath, slowly and evenly, through your nose, filling up your chest. Then exhale slowly out your mouth, emptying your chest cavity and then continuing to exhale by pressing down through your abdomen. Only when you've exhaled completely should you draw in your next slow breath.

Put on a Show!

Offer some (non-media) entertainment to the young children in your life—start with your neighborhood!—by getting theatrical. Recruit a few friends or family members, create an age-appropriate story, and write a script. Then make some simple costumes, designate a "stage," and put on a show. Puppets are always a hit with children, and the sillier the better. Oh, and don't forget the popcorn!

> YOGA IS ALL ABOUT DEEP BREATHING AND DEEP STRETCHING. THESE ARE MY FAVORITES!

Finding Your Frequency

Have you ever found yourself switching from one radio or TV channel, or Web site, to the next, never quite satisfied? What if you could have one place that played exactly what you wanted?

Being dialed in to yourself is like finding that perfect place. It's about discovering yourself and your values (yes, that's one of the three Girl Scout leadership keys!)—what interests you, defines you, moves you, and scares you. It's about exploring what you appreciate in the world and what you want to change. It's about knowing your story!

Once you know the story you want to be part of, you can start influencing the media story all around you!

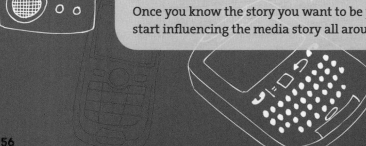

Inspiration Airwave

Inspiration is what gets you off the couch and moving! It's what allows you to be creative, accomplish your goals, and inspire others. Inspiration is what lets you be a leader! Inspiration can come from just about anywhere. What you see, hear, feel, taste, and experience can inspire you—and move you to inspire others.

Take a moment to jot down the people, places, things, or ideas that get you going—that make you jump out of bed in the morning and keep you energized all day.

Music Can inspire, Too!

{ If Media had a **BFF**, it might as well be music. }

When it comes to the media, few things are accidental. Most of what you see has been carefully chosen to make you react in a certain way—and music plays a starring role in doing just that.

Music sets A MOOD.

It gives people a way to express their thoughts and emotions. Have you ever stuck around to watch a commercial just because the music was so good? Can you remember a time when a song made you happy or excited, sad or sentimental? When was the last time music moved you to dance—even if just inside your head? *That's inspiration!*

Music is also a great EQUALIZER.

It brings people together from all parts of the world and all walks of life. With music, language barriers and cultural differences take a backseat to beat, tempo, and sentiment.

Music is also one of the greatest STRESS BUSTERS around!

1890
The first jukebox. By the 1950s, jukeboxes were commonplace in all kinds of businesses. You can still find them in some bars, old-fashioned diners, and, of course, antiques stores.

1910
Dance music is recorded for the first time. It took very heavy equipment to play it—so unlike carrying music around in your pocket these days!

MAKE YOUR OWN PLAYLIST

Mix some music for a friend or family member—particularly someone from a generation other than your own, or someone who lives far away and may not listen to the same music as you do. Afterward, ask that person to make a music mix for you. What did you discover about each other?

> DANCE MUSIC CHEERS ME UP, CLASSICAL RELAXES ME, AND SAD SONGS ARE GREAT WHEN I NEED A GOOD CRY. JUST DON'T MAKE ME SHUFFLE THEM— I'D BE A BASKET CASE!

Playlist Possibilities
Jot down your song ideas here!

1988
CDs become more popular than vinyl records and sell like hotcakes until the 2000s, when MP3 players begin stealing sales. Now more and more people have gone digital with their music. What will be the next music evolution?

Media Job Listing

Disc Jockey
A person who selects and plays recorded music for an audience. Some DJs use multiple tracks at the same time to mix sounds together, or even add their own vocals behind the music.

Background MUSIC, Anyone?

Music is used in different ways in different places.

Toward the Award

monitor

Think of commercials, ball games, and shopping malls. What is music meant to do or accomplish for each?

Track when and where you hear music—on a weekday, then on a weekend day. How do you react to it? Is the music working on you the way it's supposed to? Why or why not?

entertain

Change emotions

Change spirit

make $

A Girl Scout Melody

Music has always been an integral part of the Girl Scout experience. Sheet music was printed in handbooks, and then entire songbooks were published. Then came CDs and online music files. Remember the "Brownie Hiking Song"? Bet you can still sing every line of that! It's no surprise that so many Girl Scout songs celebrate the fundamental ideals of Girl Scouting! Some songs speak of working together; others bridge language barriers to cement the truth of universal sisterhood. And they all lighten the load on a long hike. So sing strong, sing long! (And maybe even put some singing in your MEdia Remake for the Influence award on this journey!)

CHANGE THE SOUNDTRACK

If you want to see how music is used to enhance the mood of a story, watch 15 minutes of a TV show or movie that uses a lot of music—with the sound muted. What do you notice about the movie or show that you didn't notice before?

Or simply look through a set of old pictures—of yourself as a baby or of a trip you took—while playing different types of music. Change the music every once in a while, to a driving beat, a mellow instrumental, or hip hop ...whatever you have. How did changing the soundtrack change the way you felt about what you were seeing?

Take a Media Moment

Use your MP3 player to tune out the world and tune in to music. Close your eyes and listen—really listen—to a song. You can deepen your appreciation of a song's melody, rhythm, instrumentation, and lyrics when you concentrate on what you're hearing instead of letting it waft by as background noise while you multitask on a zillion other things! How did it work out for you?

The Girl Scout Printing Press

In 1916, just four years after she founded the Girl Scouts, Juliette Gordon Low launched the group's first magazine —a tradition that continued for more than 90 years. And if you're looking for evidence that the group still relies on printed publications to inspire its members, look no further than the book you're reading right now! What inspiration are you getting from it? What does Girl Scouts want for you—and every girl?

Today's "Printing Press"

Nowadays, many people take to their computer when they want to publish something. If you had a blog, what would you post? How would you use it to express yourself and to inspire others? Use the "screen" below to make a list.

Using Your Passion to Lead

One of the greatest gifts you have as a leader is your ability to inspire others—your family, your friends, your community, the media, even the world. To inspire others is to influence them in positive ways!

Your strengths and talents are the boxes in which you wrap those gifts. They're what give character to your voice. They are directly tied to your passion, and your passion is what propels you to create change!

To be passionate about something, you don't need to be an expert at it. Knowing your talents and what you're passionate about gets you closer to the core you, to understanding that you have the building blocks of powerful talents inside you right now.

How do you know what talents you might have? And how can those talents make the world a better place? First, dial into what you like. Then determine how you can turn some of those "likes" into true talents, and apply those talents to making the world a better place!

Upload This!

Sometimes you can be too close to yourself for your own good. Get together with friends or family and ask them to name one thing you do well or something that makes you unique or special. Then return the compliment!

1981

MTV, a music video channel, goes on cable 24/7. Back then, believe it or not, they actually aired videos. Now, most of the airtime is taken up with other programming.

What I Like Best

Start by brainstorming your many interests—the things you care about, think about, and enjoy doing.

You might write down your favorite school subjects or all the numerous things that distract you from school. (Some are probably already scattered throughout the pages of this book!)

Remember, don't edit yourself. And don't judge yourself!

If you've reread a not-so-literary novel a few times, put it on the list! If you love watching gymnastics, put that on the list, too. Do you enjoy cooking, collecting bugs, identifying constellations, visiting your grandmother? Are you drawn to gossip magazines or circus performers, or the food-gathering rituals of chipmunks? Write it all down; you never know what you may learn from seeing all your interests written down in one place.

Take a look at your list.
Do any patterns emerge? Do you see an interest that you'd like to pursue further? Turning an interest into a real skill or talent—now that's exciting!

MY FAVORITES

Listing your "favorites" is another way to get a picture of your interests and yourself.

Favorite movie

Favorite book

Favorite song

Favorite place

Favorite time of day

Favorite food

Favorite person

Favorite subject

Favorite Web site

Favorite outdoor activity

Favorite indoor activity

Favorite thing about my family

Favorite thing about my school

Favorite expression

Favorite game

Favorite way to express yourself

Favorite club/organization

Ask yourself why each item was your favorite.

Do you see a pattern? For example, are all your faves related to one thing, like science, or sports, or romance? Then think about who and what influence your opinions. Your parents? Your friends? Kids at school? The media? Do the signals you get from any or all of them sway your opinions or do they make your convictions stronger? What might you do to widen your media world?

65

Turning Interests into Talents

Tomato seeds have the potential to produce countless tomatoes. But they won't grow an inch without water and sunlight.

Likewise, none of your interests can develop into full-fledged talents without some dedicated time and attention.

YOUR TALENTS

Look over all the interests and favorite things you listed and think about how you could take some (or all!) to a higher level.

If you love to draw, couldn't you draw more often? If you love to sing, couldn't you learn some new songs?

There are endless ways to hone a talent, so be creative! Remember, when you have a better handle on who you are and what interests you want to develop as you move forward in your life, it's like being on the starting line in a race to make a difference. *Ready, Set, Go for it!*

Any interest that can be enriched or deepened in some way is a potential talent in the making. Turn your interests into talents and your talents into influences—to create the reality you want to be in, and the story you want to tell!

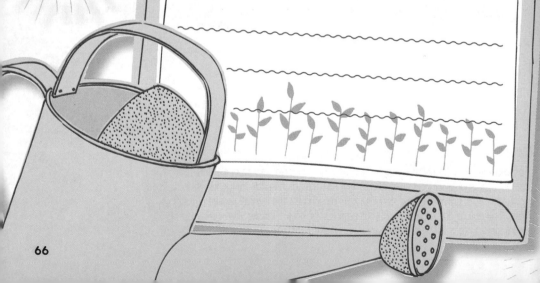

Anim-8
Morphing

To turn one image into another, animators often use a technique called "morphing" (short for metamorphosizing, the term used to describe how something changes from one thing to another, like a caterpillar to a butterfly). Here's how to create a caterpillar-to-butterfly "morph" in a simple, hand-drawn way:

(1) Start with a 24-page memo pad (staple one together from blank sheets, or tear off part of a larger pad).

(2) Wrap the top inch with tape.

(3) Draw a caterpillar on the last page, using only the bottom half of the sheet.

(4) On the first page, in the same position as the caterpillar, draw a butterfly.

(5) Working from last page to the first, draw the caterpillar changing shape, ever so slightly, page by page, until it almost matches the butterfly by the second page. The "in-betweens" are often amorphous ("without shape") drawings.

(6) Flip the pages and watch the metamorphosis take place before your watchful eyes!

Once you have the hang of this, see if you can make the Daisy Promise Center and Learning Petals "morph" into a 10-Year Award to symbolize growth in Girl Scouts. How cool is that?

Your Story, Your Change

You're just one girl, right? And your Cadette team may be small. What can a handful of girls do to change the world? After all, it's often difficult enough just deciding what to eat for breakfast!

But people are as big as their own voices. When you have something to say, and you're willing to say it, your stature suddenly changes. Think about leaders and heroes from your history books. Think about famous composers, inventors, and authors. These women and men had something to say. So, yes, you may be a girl who stands 4 feet 10 inches tall and your Cadette friends may not be much taller, but **your effect on the world can be much, much bigger than that.**

Break It Down!

As with everything in life, making yourself BIG is simply a matter of taking one step (or growing one size!) at a time.

Here's a tip:

When you've got something important you want to say, break it down. Come up with three, five, even 10 small steps you can take to get there.

And how will you know you are there? Here are some simple questions to help you recognize when you've gone from media lover to media leader:

Do you hear yourself? Your own thoughts and your own ideas?

Are other people listening to you?

Television Trailblazer

Carol Jenkins remembers her first television vividly. It had a black-and-white screen built into a huge piece of furniture called a console, and it lurked in the corner of the living room. It was the early 1950s, and her family was the first on their block in Queens, New York, to have a TV. She was mesmerized.

"I never expected to get outside of Queens," Jenkins says. "So the TV was my travel agent. It was my magic carpet. I was educated by what happened on that TV."

Some 20 years later, Jenkins' face was appearing in living rooms throughout the country. She spent most of her career as a correspondent and Emmy Award–winning anchor for various TV networks. She has since gone on to be an advocate for making women visible and powerful in the media.

As a television anchor, Jenkins blazed two new trails—the first by being female, the second by being black. When she started, women and minorities were "window dressing" and all the power positions belonged to white men. "It's startling to realize that most of the power positions still belong to white men," she says. "Only 3 percent of media's clout positions are held by women. Women and girls in this country have been conditioned to take less when it comes to the media and expect to have to fight to be included."

Sexism in the media "does not need to continue," Jenkins adds. "Women and girls need to raise their voices and complain—and make themselves heard. Being engaged in media at a young age is hugely beneficial," Jenkins says. Girls "can tell their stories…They need to know that their stories are valued."

News Anchor or Newscaster

Media Job Listing

A person who gathers or presents news stories, for either TV or radio.

1938
The first color television broadcast takes place, but color TV sets won't be available for another 10 years or so. And they weren't very affordable until the 1960s. Today's high-def, flat-screen TVs aren't cheap either. But they weigh a lot less.

1950
TV networks start airing children's programs on Saturday morning. And thank goodness! Can you imagine a world without Saturday morning cartoons?

What Bothers You?

Chances are, no TV show features a girl exactly like you. Even sitcoms designed for girls tend to be exaggerated or sensationalized.

How do these images affect your feelings and your behavior, or your friends?

Do they make you want to be impossibly thin, too?

Have you noticed how many TV characters are impossibly thin, impossibly rich, or impossibly self-confident?

Or do they make you hungry for a cheeseburger?

Do the girls in your favorite show always wear extra-skinny jeans?

Identify some things about the media that bother you—really bother you. (For Carol Jenkins, one key thing is sexism!) Look closely at an hour of TV programming, or flip through a fashion magazine or your local newspaper. Take note of all the billboards you see on your way to school. Or surf the Internet for ideas. What do you notice that gets you fired up? That's the desire to create change!

Can Video Games Change the World?

Video games aimed at saving the world instead of destroying everything in it? Seriously? Seriously! That's why Susanne Seggerman founded Games for Change—an organization that brings together students and game developers worldwide to come up with games that address big issues like poverty, human rights, education, and climate change.

Game Designer

Media Job Listing

Someone who designs gameplay by coming up with the rules and structure (levels) for games, often using animation techniques. Software programming? Yes, that, too.

1986

The Japanese firm Nintendo introduces Game Boy, a handheld gaming device. Within a few years, parents everywhere are yelling at their children, "Put that thing down and come to dinner!"

influence

Community Counts!

If you could take action in your community just by hitting a key on a computer keyboard, what issue would you choose to tackle? What cause touches your heart the most, and why?

If you surveyed your community to find out what bothers people about media—and what they'd like to change—what did they say? How can you work together to make these changes take root?

Your MEdia Remake!

Now's your chance to create the MEdia reality —*the story*—you want for yourself and other girls.

So . . . first things first. In what way do you most want to inspire others? That will help determine what you want to remake and why.

Look all around and decide on a media issue you want to tackle. Maybe it's something that turned up when you surveyed your community. Maybe it's something you've noticed that others have ignored.

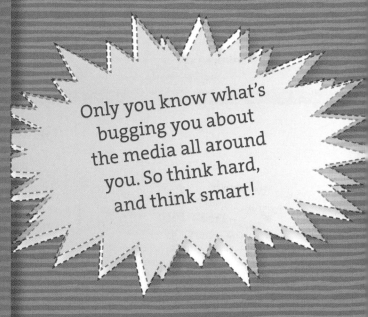

Only you know what's bugging you about the media all around you. So think hard, and think smart!

Maybe you want to...

...ban stereotypes in a popular prime-time TV show. You could storyboard or script your own episode and you could share it with students in a media studies class at your school or a local college. And you could also try sending it to the original producers.

...change an ad or ad campaign to debunk unhealthy body-image myths, expose false claims and useless products, or address a harmful advertising-related issue you've found in your community. You could create a PSA to counteract any of the above and get it aired on your local TV station.

...stop fashion spreads of unrealistic models. You could create your own real-life spread using real-life models, and share it with a group of younger girls so they can gain a better view of what "beautiful" really means. And then you could send it to the magazine's fashion editors, too.

...rewrite a popular song that's loaded with negative or anti-female lyrics. You could write your own version and get some airtime for it or pass it around online, and send it to the original writer and performer.

Or maybe...

...a blockbuster movie is way too violent or sexist, or just doesn't show women in real-life ways. You could use the "movie trailer" format, remake the story line, and then post it online for others to see!

...create a new soundtrack for an existing movie, TV show, or commercial because you think the original sends the wrong message. You could combine various kinds of music (classical, techno, pop, country) to create your new soundtrack, one that changes the mood entirely.

No matter the size of your MEdia Remake or the time you have to devote to it, you can still have an impact.

Still haven't settled on an "issue" for your Remake?
Try answering one or more of these questions.

?

I could live without seeing _____ anymore on TV, in the movies, on the Web, or in magazines.

It would be nice if I didn't have to worry about being/doing _____ just because other girls think it's cool. What does the media have to do with that?

Wouldn't it be great if there were a TV show or movie about _____.

Sound Bite

A mashup is the combination of two or more existing media files to make something new and creative.

*I am most self-conscious about my _____.
What part does the media play in that?*

?

*The stereotypes that most apply to me or someone I know and love are: _____.
Where do those stereotypes exist in media?*

Now, what issues are bubbling up for you? When you get together with your friends, compare notes and talk about what they'd like to see changed, too. Do any of their thoughts mirror yours? Could be you've got an issue!

Once you've envisioned what needs to change, build a support network and a plan of action for how you're going to put some real ME into your MEdia Remake. Follow the tips in the coming pages. But, first, keep this in mind:

A great MEdia Remake (aka your Influence project) will have you:

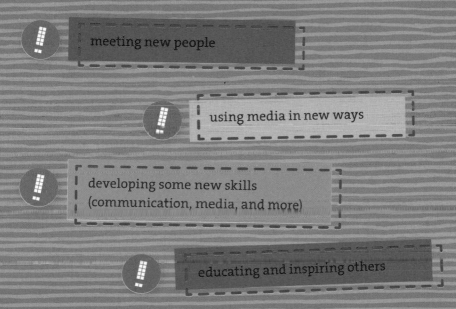

meeting new people

using media in new ways

developing some new skills (communication, media, and more)

educating and inspiring others

Why are all those things important? *They are the same things leaders do to stay on top of their game!*

And remember, your MEdia Remake can be big or small. If it's small, one way to create a big impact is to take a tip from advertisers and marketers and get your message to go viral. Use blogs, social media, or good old-fashioned word of mouth. Build a buzz, and get more and more people thinking and talking about it! You're basically giving your project some charisma—that's something leaders rely on, too!

BUILD A NETWORK TO MAKE YOUR INFLUENCE REALLY COUNT

Once you've settled on your issue and the type of media you will remake, seek out some experts, mentors, and extra hands. If you're remaking a Web page, seek out the designer of sites you admire. If you're making a PSA, get some tips from filmmakers. If you're redoing a magazine spread, speak to some editors and editorial designers.

Where to find all these people? Tap into colleges and community centers: Both students and faculty can lend a hand. So, too, can professionals in your area—the folks who work at media companies, publishing houses, film studios—and savvy amateurs who are making all kinds of creative stuff after their day jobs.

HELP DESK

When seeking support and guidance from others on your MEdia Remake, be sure to ask them:

? How would you go about this?

? What am I overlooking?

? How can I be more effective?

? Who else would you suggest I talk to?

To plan out your Remake and make sure that you and your Cadette team don't miss a beat, use all the tips and planning sheets the adult volunteer has for you.

Work the Girl Scout network, too. With million of girls, families, and volunteers in Girl Scouting, you'll find someone who knows how to do what you want to learn to do!

THEN, ZERO IN AND SELECT YOUR AUDIENCE

First, ask yourself: Who does my "influence issue" touch? Who will get the most from my MEdia Remake?

Next, ask: Of all of the people it touches, who can best help me sustain it?

Once you have those answers, you've got the makings of an audience!

The expression "Know your audience" has become well-worn wisdom for a good reason: It's so darn important! In Girl Scouts, if you don't know your audience, how can you possibly educate and inspire or advocate for others? And if you can't educate and inspire, or advocate, you're missing out on some important parts of the Take Action leadership key!

So think about who you want to reach. Who in your community would be your best audience? How big will that audience be? One person, a team, a community group? How familiar are they with your subject? Why will your audience be interested in what you have to say? What's in it for them? Remember, if you can make your audience care, then you've brought them into *your story*!

If you can, try for the original makers of the media, too! If you're trying to reach people you've never met before (like TV executives or members of the city council), you might need to do some research. Find out who they are and how they communicate. Think about what will get their attention.

Now, how are you going to get your audience to see your Remake? That's where knowing your audience comes in!

KNOW HOW TO REACH YOUR AUDIENCE

If you are presenting to...

you might ...

kids at school ...

... be funny and clever; use slang terms.

the general public ...

... ensure your language and method of communication appeal to as many groups as possible.

politicians ...

... rely on letters, phone calls, or petitions to get your point across.

people who speak a language other than your own ...

... use a translator or interpreter.

old-media executives ...

... be formal; write letters of invitation.

new-media executives ...

creative types ...

... use new media in a creative way to grab their attention.

When Flops Don't Really Fail

In the world of media, flops are commonplace—but media makers learn from their mistakes and keep moving forward.

Take Apple Inc., for example, the company that makes the wildly popular Macintosh computers, iPods, and iPhones. In 1980, just a few years after Apple was founded, it released a computer called the Apple 3, which was instantly dubbed "a catastrophe." Unattractive, hugely expensive—$8,000!—and full of design problems, the Apple 3 is now considered one of the worst computers ever built. But the company pressed on—and did it pay off! In 2009, Apple's annual sales topped $32 billion, and Fortune magazine named it the world's most admired company.

"Fun Failure"

Why is "failure" treated like a bad word? Trying new things almost always means risking failure, and that means there are loads of failures in the world! But failing doesn't have to be painful. "Fun Failure" is the concept that the fun is in the trying, not the succeeding. So let yourself fall on your face. Then pick yourself up, have a laugh, and go at it again! Keep this in mind throughout your MEdia Remake!

Putting the ME in MEdia

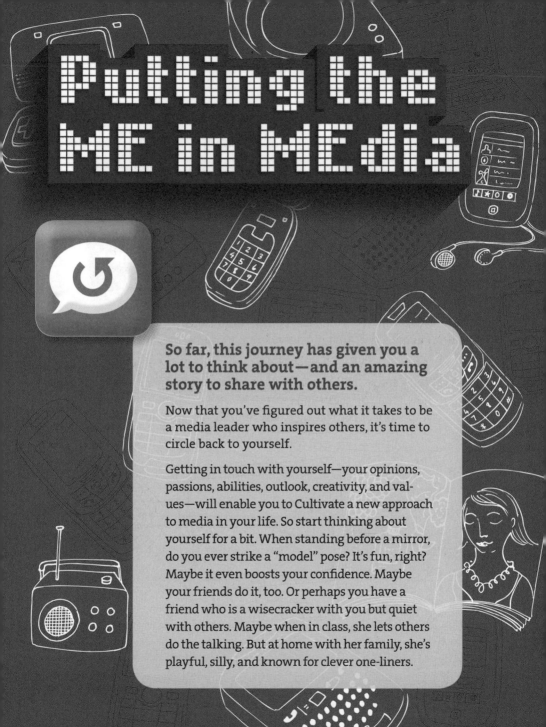

So far, this journey has given you a lot to think about—and an amazing story to share with others.

Now that you've figured out what it takes to be a media leader who inspires others, it's time to circle back to yourself.

Getting in touch with yourself—your opinions, passions, abilities, outlook, creativity, and values—will enable you to Cultivate a new approach to media in your life. So start thinking about yourself for a bit. When standing before a mirror, do you ever strike a "model" pose? It's fun, right? Maybe it even boosts your confidence. Maybe your friends do it, too. Or perhaps you have a friend who is a wisecracker with you but quiet with others. Maybe when in class, she lets others do the talking. But at home with her family, she's playful, silly, and known for clever one-liners.

It's completely natural for people to identify themselves in lots of ways and to be many ways— depending on the company they happen to be keeping at the moment.

But when you want to tell one powerful story to the world, you might feel you have to choose one voice to tell it with. Which do you choose? How do you find the "real you"? Or is it the combination of your many voices that makes you really you?

Think about yourself as a leader. Which sides of yourself get the spotlight then? List them here, and then see how many of them you can put to use when you tell your story of cultivating a new approach to MEdia!

~~~~~~

~~~~~~

~~~~~~

~~~~~~

~~~~~~

Y is for YOU

Say you were an entry in a Web-based encyclopedia that anyone could edit. What would you find under your name? What would your friends write about you? How about your family, your teachers, your Girl Scout group? What about classmates who don't know you very well? How accurate would they be? How would your entry showcase your ability as a leader?

Me

What if you wrote your own entry?
What would you write about yourself?

My Life

What if you were scripting a documentary about yourself? How would your story unfold? How would it grow as you become a Girl Scout Senior? An Ambassador?

2004

Facebook gives social media a new name. Five years later, more than 350 million people are using Facebook to share their lives and keep tabs on their friends and family.

2005

YouTube posts its first video. Today, although videos are constantly being uploaded or removed, it's estimated that well over 100 million YouTube videos exist.

Girl Scouts Makes the Hall of Fame

Have you ever caught a Hallmark Hall of Fame movie on TV? Well, one of the first Hallmark specials—which aired in 1952—was about the life of Juliette Gordon Low! It was called *Juliette Low and the Girl Scouts* and starred actress Lucile Watson as Low. The timing was not accidental. It was presented on the occasion of the Girl Scouts' 40th anniversary.

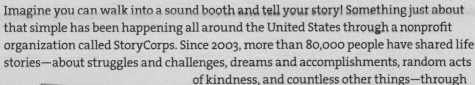

Imagine you can walk into a sound booth and tell your story! Something just about that simple has been happening all around the United States through a nonprofit organization called StoryCorps. Since 2003, more than 80,000 people have shared life stories—about struggles and challenges, dreams and accomplishments, random acts of kindness, and countless other things—through

recorded conversations. This oral history project is preserved at the Library of Congress. Some stories are even broadcast on public radio!

How do you think people decide what story to share with the world? What would you share?

FINDING YOUR FEET AND TESTING YOUR GUT

"Challenge" can be a scary word. You, like most people, probably reside in a comfort zone bordered by your own fears. That is a good thing when the fears are legitimate, such as a fear of being physically hurt. But how much of your comfort zone is created by fears of things like failure, embarrassment, loneliness, or change?

Committing to a challenge—no matter how big or small—expands the space of your comfort zone. The more challenges you take on, the more courageous a leader you become.

Name something your own thoughts or insecurities have prevented you from doing, whether it's making a four-course dinner for your family or wearing that new hat you bought three months ago. Now step outside your comfort zone, and give it a try.

How'd it go?
Tell the story of your experience here:

10 Great Ways to Challenge Yourself

1 Enter a contest.

2 Try out for a sport.

3 Make a new friend.

4 Take up a new hobby.

5 Join a new club.

6 Give a speech.

7 Organize a gathering (start a group, throw a party!).

8 Say "I'm sorry" to someone you hurt (even if that person hurt you, too).

9 Confront a problem you're having with a friend, family member, or someone else you know.

10 Say "no" to a friend who is pressuring you to do something you shouldn't do or don't want to do.

Try one or, better yet, try them all!

Art as Natural as Nature

You'd think that people would look at Jennifer Steinkamp's art and think of nature, but it's really the other way around.

"They look at real nature and then they think of my work. It's kind of nice," says Steinkamp, who uses computers and software to create images of nature that look real and lyrical but actually move in unusual, unnatural ways.

Her "Dervish," for example, shows projections of trees with wildly twirling branches, inspired by the whirling ritual practiced by some Islamic priests known as dervishes. "Florence Nightingale" features rows of computer-animated flowers that bob, sway, and swirl in a mesmerizing dance.

Steinkamp, a professor of design and media arts at the University of California, Los Angeles, sometimes places projectors close to the ground so viewers cast shadows on her images. Or she uses sensors, which are activated by viewers as they move around, to change the images being seen. In "The Sky is Falling," she created a way for viewers to see pictures they draw transformed into images of falling cloth shown on a giant LED screen mounted on the side of a building.

Some of Steinkamp's twirling trees honor her favorite teachers. One of them honors her first-grade teacher, Miss Znerold, who once told the future artist that she made the best sponge trees in the class.

Dialing into Artwork

Artist Katie Holten created an installation known as "Tree Museum" by choosing 100 trees in a New York City neighborhood and putting phone numbers on the trees for people to call.

When they called, they heard what others from the neighborhood—rappers, poets, children, experts—had to say about the trees. Or they heard the sounds of animals, insects, even the trees themselves!

Of course, phones can be used in artwork in other ways, too. They might be materials in sculpture or performance art. Some artists in China, Europe, the United States, and elsewhere are even using the tones of cell phones to create music!

Look at the phone nearest to you right now. What kind of art could you make with it?

Gimme a C!

Now, it's time
to challenge yourself to
Cultivate better use of media in your
own life. There are plenty of ways to do it.

You can commit to saying no to TV stereotypes (and shutting off the TV whenever they appear).

You can keep making media yourself that reflects your values.

You can keep talking back to media makers about what matters to you.

But what exactly will be your personal ongoing commitment? To figure that out, jot down what has inspired you most along this journey. What opened your eyes, surprised you, made you mad, or made you think, and made you want to create?

1. _____
2. _____
3. _____

So what ended up on your list? And what on that list speaks to you the most? Just remember: No matter where your ideas come from, this challenge is for you, so the choice is up to you.

1914
The first transcontinental telephone call. It would be another 65 years before telemarketers started bugging people in the middle of dinner!

1974
The word "Internet" enters the lexicon, although most people won't be surfing the Web for another 20 years.

Cultivate
Commitment

Toward the Award

cultivate

Once you've decided, write your commitment in one clear sentence:

I commit to ﹏﹏﹏﹏﹏﹏﹏﹏﹏﹏﹏﹏﹏﹏﹏﹏﹏﹏﹏﹏

Now, figure out how you will get that commitment started!

Keep in mind that as you Cultivate this personal media commitment, you may actually be cultivating change in the world around you. Your actions can inspire others to act, too! Inspiring others—that's exactly what leaders do!

To get your commitment going, use your media talents (you know best what they are!). Express what you want to change in a creative way, maybe even through new media you've learned about on this journey.

Say you've committed not to having magazines around that will send unwanted messages to your younger sister. You might create a fun magazine for her as a gift!

Suppose you want to speak up when movies depict girls in a way that's hurtful. You might design an invitation for girls to join a movie critique group.

Suppose you've committed to finding a way to be healthy and more active instead of sitting in front of the TV or computer so much. You might make up an "I'm not sitting in front of the TV or my computer" dance!

Using your talents to Cultivate change is just one more great way to be a media leader. Fill out the Award Tracker on page 95 and make your commitment official! Then start cultivating! Spread your story!

Share your commitment with your Girl Scout friends and others. You'll grow as a media leader as you inspire others to follow in your footsteps and make changes in their use of media, too. And maybe you can get that MIC of yours blasting so that your story will go viral and inspire even more people!

MEDIA AWARD

For the Monitor Award

To earn the award, complete at least three of these activities, plus
take part in the community media activity with your Cadette team.

What I did	What I learned
☑ Slice the Media Pie	
☐ Message Overload	
☑ Take It Apart	
Dip into the Dip!	
☐ Messages in the Girl Scout Law	
☒ Be a Spam Blocker!	
☑ Stereotype Search	
Background Music, Anyone?	
Community Media Activity	What we learned:

Community Media Activity
What we did: survey
survey

TRACKER

Toward the Award  monitor

What I accomplished

Ideas we used toward our MEdIa Remake:

For the Influence Award

Now that you've investigated the media that's all around you, you have plenty of ideas—positive and negative—about the media, and probably some ideas about the story you'd like to change through your MEdia Remake!

The media issues I identified:

What not to do online

My media interests/talents-in-the-making are:

My interests/talents could be used to inspire and lead others by:

MEdia Remake

The media my team and I chose to remake is

My team and I are remaking it by

I am using my talents by

The impact I hope to have is

What I hope to learn is

We shared our MEdia remake with

Here's what happened

For the Cultivate Award

I, _____ , as a media lover and media maker, will Cultivate the following MEdia challenge for the good of myself (and maybe even the world!):

~~~~~~

~~~~~~

~~~~~~

This represents my ongoing commitment to being a media leader!

I have shared my commitment by:

~~~~~~

~~~~~~

Now, Take the MIC!

For having only five letters, "media" is an awfully BIG word, isn't it? People use it in trillions of ways, in gazillions of places, and there is so much of it to absorb and enjoy.

Flip back through this journey, and you'll be reminded of all you have already absorbed! You'll be reminded of how you **Connected** with others...

...how you, as media leader, can **Take Action** by educating and inspiring others toward the media reality you want to live in. . .

...and how, through media, you can **Discover** so much about yourself and your values.
Think back on all that media can do for you, and all that media can help you accomplish!

With your new awareness of media, you can make the world a little better, a little more real...you can make the world's story a little more like *your story*!

So continue on as a media leader! Could you now use media to lead people far beyond the reaches of their wildest imaginations?

Bet you could! There's just one thing left to do: *Celebrate!*

So go ahead: Step up to the MIC and tell your story.

**The MIC is yours and you deserve it.
Now keep on using it!**